D1391841

PET OWNER'S GUIDE TO THE
BEARDED COLLIE

Brenda White

RINGPRESS

ABOUT THE AUTHOR

Brenda White was bought up in an animal-loving family and her childhood was spent caring for a variety of cats and dogs, as well as looking after ponies, orphan lambs and guinea pigs. She had always wanted a 'shaggy dog', and it was when watching television she discovered the Bearded Collie – a pedigree breed with a wonderful temperament and true 'shaggy dog' appeal. Brenda purchased her first Beardie in 1973 and has been involved with the breed ever since; breeding, showing and judging them at the highest level. To date, she has bred nine British Champions, and she campaigned Cassie – Ch. Pottersdale Classic of Moonhill – to win Crufts Supreme Best in Show in 1989.

ACKNOWLEDGEMENTS

My thanks to photographers Amanda Bulbeck and Michael Trafford, and to those who supplied photos of their dogs, especially L. Dumbrell, D. Barley, W. Rawson, B. Calloway, E. Gallatly, G. Ellis-Brown, R. Gentle, T. Pool, M. Baker, J. Tucker and T. Paakkanen.

Published by Ringpress Books Limited,
PO Box 8, Lydney, Gloucestershire,
GL15 6YD, United Kingdom.

First published 1998
©1998 Ringpress Books Limited. All rights reserved

ISBN 1 86054 087 2

Printed and bound in Italy

CONTENTS

TRAINING YOUR BEARDIE

5

GROOMING

6

HEALTH CARE

7

Quinbury Stormdrifter at Runival CD
Ex: The Bearded Collie is ideally
suited to his work on the hills, with his
shaggy coat providing protection
against the worst of the weather.

Introducing The Bearded Collie

Tracing the history of the Bearded Collie is not easy. References dating back to 1840 emphasise particular characteristics which identify these dogs as a separate breed, but unlike spaniels and hounds, which are depicted in works of art and books, Bearded Collies were not owned by noblemen or landed gentry. Had they been, their ancestry and history would be on record, but these were working dogs, owned by herdsmen and shepherds.

There is no doubt that Beardies, as they are affectionately known, are descended from a family of shaggy sheepdogs that were found all over Europe. This common stock probably came to Britain by

Sunbree Such Delight: A combination of self-assurance and intelligence makes the Beardie a reliable worker, driving and gathering both cattle and sheep.

way of war or trade, and was to be found with the Celtic peoples on the fringes of the country. Before Beardies evolved as a pure breed, farmers would have mated one good working dog to another with an equally strong working instinct, irrespective of looks, and it is from this type of dog that Beardies evolved into one of three offshoots of the European shaggy sheepdog developed in Britain. The other two were the Old English Sheepdog and the Welsh Grey. This latter breed has only recently disappeared.

The Bearded Collie was bred to gather and drove, which requires running and barking. He should not be confused with the Border Collie, who works silently and is used for rounding up the flock or herd. A Bearded Collie, good at his job, would have been classed as a 'noisy worker' – a desirable trait. Before the days of mass transport, dogs were used to drove cattle and sheep long distances 'on the hoof' to market. The Beardie was often seen at Smithfield market in London and, in fact, was once known as the 'Smithfield Collie'.

He was also used as a hillworker, as his agility and surefootedness, together with a thick skin and shaggy weatherproof coat, meant that he could work in the worst weather, over any terrain. Great intelligence, combined with self-assurance and independence, made him an ideal working partner for the shepherd or drover. The Beardie was capable of being sent off on a task alone, returning a few days later when his work was complete. As modern transport systems were developed, livestock was sent to market in lorries and trains, and the work of the Bearded Collie began to disappear.

THE MODERN BEARDIE

Unless a particular breed is taken into the show ring when its work declines, the breed begins to die

Balmaeneil Scott: This is how Beardies looked at the turn of the century.

out. Historically, pedigree dogs are a somewhat recent development, and it is only when Breed Standards are laid down by enthusiasts that certain traits evolve. In the show ring, judges assess how closely each dog conforms to the physical properties outlined in the Breed Standards acknowledged by Kennel Clubs throughout the world.

At the turn of the century, Mrs Cameron Miller was showing Bearded Collies, and a photograph of her handsome Balmaeneil Scott appears in *Hutchinson's Dog Encyclopaedia*, giving us a good idea of how the breed looked at that time.

In 1912 the Bearded Collie Club was founded in Edinburgh by J. Russell Greig, CBE, PhD, MRCVS, FRSE. However, with the outbreak of the First World War, the club petered out. In 1944, by chance, the late Mrs G.O. Willison acquired a chocolate and white Bearded Collie puppy, who was subsequently registered as Jeannie of Bothkennar, the foundation bitch of the Bothkennar kennels.

Mrs Willison was smitten by the uncanny intelligence and wonderful character of Jeannie and set about finding a suitable mate

Eng. Am. Can. Ch. Sammara Standing Ovation. The modern Beardie still bears a marked resemblance to its early ancestors.

for her. In 1949, on the beach at Hove, in Sussex, she saw a grey, shaggy dog being exercised by his lady owner. This lady had bought the dog from a farmer in North Devon, but, as she was planning to move into a flat, she was hoping to find a country home for him. He returned home with Mrs Willison two days later, and was registered with the Kennel Club as Bailie of Bothkennar. Bailie was mated with Jeannie and it is from this pair that all pedigree Bearded Collie puppies born today are descended.

Thanks to Mrs Willison's untiring energy, the breed went from strength to strength. She encouraged Bearded Collie enthusiasts to show and breed from their stock, then searched out Beardies that were true to type and registered them with the Kennel Club and the Scottish Kennel Club. When Mrs Willison's health began to fail in the winter of 1963-1964, her famous kennel of Bothkennar Bearded Collies, that she had worked so hard to establish, had to be disbanded. But all was not lost, as the Bothkennar Beardies were placed in the safe hands of other enthusiasts who continued to breed from the bloodlines established by Mrs Willison. These 'minders of the breed' have given those of us, all over the world, who have the pleasure of owning a Bearded Collie, the truly delightful dogs they are today.

THE 'PERFECT' BEARDIE

Every registered breed is judged in the show ring against a Breed Standard, which is a written blueprint describing the 'perfect' dog. Of course, there is no such thing – but the judge's task is to assess all the entries and award the highest honours to the dogs that, in their opinion, come closest to the ideal.

In terms of appearance, the Bearded Collie Breed Standard stipulates the following points:

GENERAL APPEARANCE

The Bearded Collie should be a lean, active dog who possesses the nature of a steady, intelligent working dog. Beardies should not be short-legged, and, although strongly made, they should not look too heavy. It should be possible to see plenty of daylight under the body.

HEAD: The head should be broad and flat, with a strong muzzle, and should be in proportion to body size. The pigmentation of nose, lips and eye rims should be a solid colour, without spots or patches, and should follow the coat colour.

The eyes should tone in with the coat colour. They should be large, set widely apart, with a soft and affectionate expression.

The ears are medium-sized and droop to the side of the head. They lift at the base when the dog is alert, which increases the apparent breadth of the skull, but the set-on should not be above the top of the skull.

The teeth should be large and white – and a complete scissor bite is preferred (i.e. upper teeth closely overlapping lower teeth). A level bite is tolerated but undesirable.

BODY: The Beardie is longer in the back than height to withers. Ideally, dogs should measure 53-56 cms (21-22 ins), and bitches 51-53 cms (20-21 ins). There should be plenty of room for the heart and lungs in the long, deep ribcage. The loin area should be strong.

The neck is of moderate length – slightly arched and muscular, flowing into shoulders which slope well back.

The legs should be straight with good bone. The pasterns should be flexible but not weak. Both legs and feet are covered with shaggy hair, including between the pads.

Feet should be oval, with toes well-arched and close together and soles well-padded.

The hindquarters are well-muscled with good second thighs. Hocks are low-set and strong, and stifles are well-bent, but matching the angle of the shoulder blade in

In the show ring, the Bearded Collie is assessed against the Breed Standard – the written blueprint of the 'perfect' dog.

order to keep the animal correctly balanced.

The tail is set low and is long enough for the end of the bone to reach at least point of hock. While standing or walking, the tail is carried low with an upward swirl at the tip, this may be extended at speed. The tail should not be carried curled over the back.

MOVEMENT: The Bearded Collie should cover the ground with supple, smooth, long-reaching, effortless strides. This movement is a joy to watch in a well-balanced dog.

COAT: The Beardie has a double coat. The undercoat is thick, furry and close; the outer coat is harsh, strong and shaggy. A slight wave is permissible, but the coat should never be woolly or curly. It should be long enough to enhance the natural body lines, but not be too long as to obscure it. The hair on the bridge of the nose is more sparse. The lower lips, the cheeks and under-chin have more coat and this increases in length to form the typical beard.

COLOUR: Beardies can be all shades of grey, reddish fawn, black, blue, brown and sandy –

with or without white markings. When white markings occur they are on the foreface, a blaze on the skull, on the tip of the tail, on the chest, legs and feet. If white is round the collar, the roots of white hair should not extend behind the shoulder. White markings are not desirable on the outside of the hindlegs above the hocks. If the dog is a tri-colour it can have tan marking on the eyebrows, inside the ears, on the cheeks, under the root of the tail, and on the legs where white joins the main body colour.

THE BEARDIE CHARACTER

Some modern-day Beardies are still used for working sheep and cattle, and it is a joy to see them using the natural instincts with which they were born. However, the majority are owned first and foremost as family pets. It must be borne in mind that, even if they are not worked, their strong hereditary characteristics will not just disappear into thin air. One of the ways in which the natural working instinct comes to the fore is when the family is out walking – your Beardie will take great delight in keeping his 'flock' together by running from the pace-setters to the one or two who may be lagging behind, endeavouring to get everyone closer together.

Bearded Collies can be boisterous. On the whole, they are self-assured extroverts and possess an uncanny intelligence. They thrive on human companionship and want, very much, to be included in the family.

If dogs can have a sense of humour, Beardies do. Should they catch you smiling at their antics when you catch them up to mischief, they will do it even more! They can also be very gentle, and will understand your every mood – knowing when it is appropriate to keep a low profile, or when it would be a good time to come to you for affection.

Do not buy a Bearded Collie if it is to be left alone for hours on end, whether in your home or in a kennel. In my experience, Beardies that spend a lot of time on their own become destructive and noisy or lacklustre and dispirited. They are active dogs who need companionship, mental stimulation and plenty of free-running exercise.

Some breeds of dog hate even to get their feet wet, but this is certainly not the case with Beardies. They love to get into water to cool off during exercise and are not fussy if it is a swim in the sea or river, a quick dip in a cattle trough, or a paddle in a muddy wallow. Even during a country walk on a hot summer day, do not be lulled into a false sense of security that, today, there will be no Beardie cleaning-up process when you arrive home – they are like a piece of willow and seem to find water wherever they may be. On many occasions I have seen my Beardies stand and sniff the air, then look at each other as if to say "Can you smell that water? OK, I'll race you there", and with speed, agility and grace, off they go, coats flowing, over the horizon. On return, they are, at best, wet through but, more often than not, completely covered in muddy ringlets and, having achieved their aim, are now ready to get back into the car for the journey home.

The perfect end to a walk!

2 Choosing A Beardie

Anyone thinking of buying a dog needs to consider whether a particular breed will fit in with the family's circumstances, work commitments, and way of life. All breeds have their own particular characteristics and possess hereditary factors that enable them to carry out the task for which they were originally bred. Even if a dog is not used for the purpose for which it was developed, those hereditary characteristics remain strong, and affect its character in everyday life.

Bearded Collies grow a lovely, weatherproof, shaggy coat, which certainly adds to their appeal, and was necessary for their original work, but a considerable amount of time must be spent on grooming in order to keep the coat healthy and free from too much matting. They shed a certain amount of hair, but certainly not as much as a Labrador or a Golden Retriever. Debris also collects on the coat, so

Beardies are definitely not for the ultra-houseproud.

It may prove very useful to attend a show where several breeds are being exhibited, as it will then be possible to see the dogs, chat to owners and breeders, and be sure that a Bearded Collie is the right breed for you to be buying. You could also enquire about attending a breed club event in your area.

FINDING A BREEDER

Your national Kennel Club will be able to give you details of registered breed clubs of Bearded Collies in your area, and you can contact a club secretary for the names and addresses of your nearest breeders. Some breeders advertise puppies for sale in the various monthly dog magazines which are available from most large newsagents.

It is always a good idea to visit one or two breeders, so that you can meet the dogs at home, and

When you visit a breeder, assess the adults as well as the puppies.

perhaps join them for a walk to get a real feel for the breed. Having located a reputable breeder, telephone and make an appointment to visit him or her, and the Beardies, at home. Please be sure to keep the appointment, or give plenty of notice if you have to change it, as the breeder is giving up at least one or two hours to discuss their beloved breed, and will no doubt have spent quite a lot of time brushing the dogs, sorting out photos of Beardies at various stages of growth, and making sure refreshments are available. All this takes up valuable time, and it may be that the dogs will have to wait until the visit is over before they have a good walk.

It is a wise precaution to spend enough time with hairy dogs to find out whether anyone in the family may be asthmatic and prove to be allergic to Beardie hair, or to the dust particles that come off even the most thoroughly groomed dog. It is heartbreaking for all concerned if a dog has to be returned to the breeder because a family member is allergic to its hair. It would also be a good idea to write down the questions you would like to ask, prior to the visit, as there will be so much to learn that you may well forget to ask about a very important point. Go armed with pen and paper, so that you can make notes – you will find it impossible to retain all the infomation you are given about the breed.

Having visited one or two

breeders or chatted to exhibitors at shows, you will now be in a better position to know which bloodlines you are looking for and whether you want a Beardie as a pet and companion, a show dog, or to compete with in Obedience or Agility trials. Temperament is one of the strongest inherited characteristics, so make sure that both the sire and the dam of the litter from which you wish to book a puppy have temperaments that make them neither too shy, nor too extrovert.

DOG OR BITCH

The next step is to decide whether you want a dog or a bitch. I have owned both sexes and find little difference in their personalities, both being equally loyal and companionable. It may be argued that dogs do not have the mood swings that affect some bitches during their breeding cycle. If you take on a bitch, you will have to cope with their seasons (on average every six months) and make sure they are kept away from male dogs at this time. If you do not intend to breed from your bitch you may consider having her neutered. This is usually done around three months after the second season, when she is fully

mature. Ask your vet for advice.

Dogs are slightly taller than bitches. They have more bone, and are consequently heavier and a little bigger all round. As a rough guide, I would call a Bearded Collie a knee-height dog. Males may be liable to wander, especially if they pick up the scent of a bitch in season, but you can avoid the problem by having a secure house and garden. Should your dog pick up the scent of a bitch in season while he is being exercised, put him on his lead and keep him away from that exercise area for a week or so.

Most Bearded Collie dogs are gentle and easy to live with, but, if you find that, as your dog matures, he has a tendency to the anti-social behaviour of mounting visitors' legs, or cushions, he should be reprimanded, in order to correct the problem in the early stages. If he does persist, then neutering may prove to be a sensible option. Ask your vet for advice.

THE SHOW BEARDIE

If you specifically want a show Beardie, you need to contact a breeder who has a good track record of producing stock with excellent conformation and movement, which are true to breed type. A puppy with show potential will have a good head, correct conformation and mouth, and the right markings. It will have overall balance and a certain personality that takes your eye. Watch the puppies trotting around and you will be able to spot the best movers. A puppy of six to seven weeks of age that moves well will always do so. However, you can never guarantee how young stock will turn out. All the breeder can do is strive to produce animals that are sound, with nice temperaments and the potential to be good examples of their breed.

Beardies come in a range of colours: these two brown Beardies are pictured with their slate-coloured mother.

COAT AND COLOUR

The next consideration is what colour Beardie you would like to own – that is, if you are fortunate enough to have a choice! Keep an open mind until the litter arrives, and make any decisions when you go to visit the puppies a few weeks later. It is the Beardie's shaggy appearance that attracts many people to the breed. However, such a coat is not low-maintenance, so it is important that you understand what you are taking on.

The Bearded Collie has a double coat. The undercoat is furry, soft and close; the outer coat is flat, harsh, strong and shaggy. This outer coat can be slightly wavy, but not curly or woolly. There should be enough coat on an adult Beardie to provide a protective jacket. Bitches tend to grow a heavier coat after they have been spayed, as they cease to go through hormonal changes.

Bearded Collies go through several coat changes as they mature which, for the novice owner or enthusiast, can prove rather confusing. The colour of a Beardie at birth, and as registered with the Kennel Club, is the colour it should be referred to as an adult.

There are four main coat colours in Beardies, plus tri-colour markings, and it is possible to get all of the colours in one litter. The four colours are Slate, Blue, Brown, and Fawn.

SLATE: Born black. Black nose and pigment. Ideally, dark brown eyes. Coat colour may stay black, or may go quite pale and then darken again to a shade of grey between two and two-and-a-half years of age. Whatever shade of black or grey the adult coat is, one can determine that this dog was born Slate, as it has black nose and pigment.

BLUE: (a dilute colour of Slate): Born grey. Grey nose and pigment. Eyes generally brown/grey/blue mix and should

Slate: Born black – the coat may stay black or lighten to dark grey.

Blue: Born grey, the coat becomes paler, ending up as blue/grey.

tone with the coat colour. Blues generally pale out quite a lot during adolescence and, in fact, they can look rather washed-out in colour. As adults, their coat colour settles down to a shade of blue/grey.

Adult Slates and Blues can, in some cases, look very similar in coat colour, but the nose pigment determines the colour they were born.

BROWN: Generally born chocolate brown. Dark brown nose and pigment. Ideally dark

Brown: Born chocolate brown, the adult coat can be any shade of brown ranging from mahogany to ginger.

brown eyes. In most cases coat lightens at about 12–18 months and, at this stage, they can look almost blonde. At two-and-a-half to three years of age, the adult coat comes through and the Beardie will be a shade of brown, ranging from mahogany through to sand or ginger.

FAWN: (a dilute colour of Brown). Born beige. Will have lighter colour pigment than a Brown and the eyes are generally more yellow/brown. I have seen some Fawns with lovely dark brown eyes and strong pigment. Fawns tend to pale out a great deal in coat colour and, at about one year old, it can prove difficult to differentiate between any white markings and the main body coat colour. In time the body coat will darken slightly but will always be a sandy/cream colour.

As with Slates and Blues, Browns and Fawns can be confused, so check the nose pigment to determine whether the Beardie was born Brown or Fawn.

Tri-colour markings are acceptable with any of the four main coat colours. These tan markings can be on the eyebrows, inside ears, on cheeks, under the root of the tail and on the leg where the white markings join the

Fawn: Born beige, the adult will be sandy/cream in colour.

main colour. A Bearded Collie may have the minimum of white Collie markings and still be correctly marked, but too much white would be classed as mismarking.

If your Beardie is to be purely a pet and companion, or you wish to work it in Obedience or Agility, it does not matter if his markings are not ideal. However, if you wish to show or breed from your Beardie, colour and marking should be taken into account when choosing your puppy.

ASSESSING THE LITTER

I do not like too many visitors until a litter of puppies is about four weeks old. By this age they are being weaned, are up on their feet, and their characters are starting to develop. The dam deserves a few weeks of peace and quiet to rear her precious babies.

When you go to visit the puppies, the dam should be clean, well-groomed and in good condition. The puppies should smell clean and be free of fleas and lice. They should have clean ears and bottoms and their toenails should have been cut. Even at four to five weeks, they will have been wormed twice and should look nice, chunky, substantial pups. When picked up gently, they should feel solid. A light puppy with a distended stomach may be carrying a worm burden.

Having spent many hours with the puppies, an experienced

Watch the puppies playing – this will tell you a lot about their characters and the pecking order within the litter.

breeder will be able to assess their individual characters and be able to help choose the right puppy for you. The ideal puppy has a middle-of-the-road temperament, being neither too shy, nor too bossy, and takes everything in his stride. It is possible to test the temperaments of puppies at seven weeks, by setting simple little tests for them to do. I have had puppies tested, but the tests have not revealed anything that I had not already percieved by spending time with the pups and getting to know them individually.

Very often, I find the puppy chooses the owner, rather than the other way around! I always do my very best to ensure that prospective owners get to own the puppy they fall in love with – and that the puppy gets to live with the family he has taken a liking to. Hopefully, they will be together for many happy years. Do not let your heart rule your head and, if you feel that there is not a suitable puppy in the litter that you have gone to see, be patient until the right one does come along, perhaps from another breeder. If you make a firm booking for a puppy and live near enough to the breeder, it may be possible to call and see your puppy once or twice more before it is ready to leave home.

It is never a good idea to buy two puppies at the same time, as it proves very difficult to train them. If you decide to get another Beardie to keep the first one company, it is advisable to wait until the first one is 12–18 months

Resist the temptation of buying two puppies together, as they will prove very difficult to train.

old, when you will know some of the pitfalls, which should make rearing and training the second puppy a little easier. Also, you will find that the first one will help to train the second – for example, if you call the older one, the younger should follow close on his heels and will soon learn the command "Come". Bearded Collies are very addictive, and most owners eventually have at least two.

Do not buy a puppy when you are expecting a human addition to the family. It is far too much work to cope with a new baby and try to train a young puppy at the same time. The workload and attention necessary for raising either will be somewhat easier to cope with if there is a gap of, say,

18 months between whichever arrives first.

OLDER OR RESCUE DOG

Rather than buy a puppy, you may wish to take on an older dog or a dog who needs re-homing. Some breeders keep two puppies from a litter before deciding which one to retain. Eventually, they may be looking for a good home for one of them, who could be 6–18 months old. At this age, although still a young dog, your Beardie will be beyond the baby-puppy and teething stage.

You may wish to contact Breed Rescue (details from a breed club secretary or your national Kennel Club) to see if there is a Beardie needing a kind, loving home, due to unfortunate circumstances.

PREPARATIONS

Once you have booked your puppy, there will probably be a few weeks before it is old enough to leave its home and come to join your family. Make the most of this time to prepare for the arrival of the puppy and collect together the necessary equipment, toys, and food that you are going to need.

If there is a large championship dog show being held in your area, you will find stall-holders who will sell just about everything you need for a dog. A visit to one of these, prior to your puppy arriving home, would not only be a fun day out for you and your family, but you can go home with everything you need.

COLLAR AND LEAD

There are many types of collars and leads manufactured for dogs. Always remember that your Beardie will only be as safe as his collar and lead, so be sure that these are kept in good condition, fitted correctly and that regular checks are made on buckles, clasps and stitching. If any wear is evident, replace the item immediately.

FLAT OR ROLLED LEATHER COLLARS

One cannot go far wrong with a good-quality leather collar, which has a metal or brass buckle. The collar should be fitted neither too tight, nor so loose that the dog can slip it if he pulls backwards when frightened.

Buy a leather lead of a length that suits you. I like a longish lead, so that, if I am jogging my Beardies, they can be far enough in front that my feet do not catch their hocks as we go along.

PUPPY COLLAR AND LEAD

For a puppy I would recommend that you buy a woven nylon collar. These are soft and have a metal buckle, the spike of which can be pushed through the nylon webbing at any point on the collar which fits the puppy comfortably, without being too loose or too tight. These collars are very useful over the weeks when the puppy goes through rapid growth. Let the puppy wear the collar for short periods each day to get used to the feel of it. A nylon lead can be purchased to match the collar.

IDENTIFICATION

By law, no dog should be allowed to run free in a public place without some means of identification. I always have identification tags attached to my

Items to buy include safe toys, chews, a ceramic water bowl and a food bowl.

Beardies' leather collars which remain on them at all times when they are loose. On one side of the ID tag I have my surname engraved and, on the other, my home telephone number and also my mobile number. That way, if the dog is lost and I am out looking for it, anyone finding the dog has a better chance of contacting me.

Always ensure that your dog has a collar with an ID tag on when you take him out in the car. If there should be an accident, the dog could get out of the car and run away in fright. You can also consider tattooing, or having an Identichip inserted under the dog's skin. Ask your vet about these two options.

TOYS

There are some excellent toys available which have been specifically designed for dogs. Do buy a selection to keep your puppy occupied and on which he can chew. Toys which have a squeaker inside can often cause annoyance, especially to another dog in the family, but the squeaker can easily be removed and the puppy can still play with his chosen toy. Balls to play with should be tennis ball size, or larger. Anything smaller could lodge in a dog's throat, which would cause it to choke to death.

FOOD BOWL

I find that stainless steel bowls are ideal for food. They are hard-wearing, easy to keep clean, and can be sterilised.

WATER BOWL

Given the choice of plastic, stainless steel or china, my dogs will always go to a china bowl for a drink, which makes me wonder if the water in the other bowls gets a plastic or steel taste to it. So, needless to say, I use a china bowl for the dogs' drinking water. Be sure that your dog has fresh water available at all times and that you change the water in the bowls at least twice a day.

I use a 'non-spill' water bowl in the back of my car when travelling. These are made of plastic and are available at dog shows and events, or from good pet stores.

Useful tip: If your dog paddles in his water bowl, place his own bowl, filled with water, inside an empty plastic washing-up bowl. Should he still try to paddle, the water which gets spilled will go into the outer bowl and not all over the floor. Puppies do usually grow out of this habit!

GROOMING

If you take on a Bearded Collie, you will need brushes and combs to keeps his coat in good order. The equipment needed and tips on grooming can be found in Chapter Six.

BEDS

Rigid plastic, dog basket-shaped beds are ideal. They are easy to keep clean and some are now made with air-holes in the base, so that the bedding does not sweat, should your dog go to bed a little damp at times. Buy one that is large enough for an adult Beardie, with a base 85cm long, and measuring 95cm at the top. Your

There is a wide range of beds to choose from. The rigid, plastic type (centre) is the most practical.

puppy may seem lost in it at first but he will soon grow into it.

Foam beds covered in material are washable and also come in the shape of a dog basket. Do not invest in one of these until your puppy is beyond his teething stage, otherwise it may not last very long. These beds are ideal to take with you when you go away as they can either be rolled up in a corner of the car, or put in the back for the dog to sleep in while travelling, which is what my Beardies love to do. On arrival, if the dog bed is taken into the house or hotel, my dog knows we are staying and will settle more quickly. When the bed goes back into the car, it is a sign to the dog that we will soon be on the move again. Make sure the bed is put in a draught-free place.

BEDDING
You may wish to use blankets, or similar, for your pet's bedding. However, the favoured bedding for dogs these days is manufactured from man-made fibre which looks very like sheep-skin and is also soft, thick and warm to the touch. It has a woven back to the fabric, is washable,

hard-wearing and comes in various colours. Any moisture goes through the fabric so that the dog lying on it should stay warm, cosy and dry, making it ideal for dogs of all ages. It is available under several trade names and the quality and price will vary according to the make. Most breeders rear their puppies on this bedding, so you will be able to make enquiries about it when you go to see your puppy.

INDOOR KENNEL
Wire folding kennels are becoming very popular. They are useful pieces of equipment and it is well worth investing in one of good quality, which should last for many years. Buy one that is large enough for an adult Beardie to lie down or sit, and to stand up in comfortably. They can be supplied

An indoor folding kennel will prove invaluable.

with either a side or end door opening to suit your requirements and also have a plastic tray which fits in the base. Not only can they be used in the home, but they can be folded flat for transportation and taken with you if you go away.

The folding kennel will have many uses but it should be remembered that it must never be used to keep a Beardie in constantly, and never used as a place of punishment. It is purely for making life a little easier, with benefits for both dog and owner. Used correctly, your Beardie will have pleasant associations with the kennel. He will look upon it as his 'den' and safe haven. You will find, as time goes by, if the door of his kennel is always left open, he will take himself inside for a rest whenever he feels the need to get away from it all, to find peace and quiet. He can then enjoy an undisturbed rest, and will not get under anyone's feet while doing so.

STAIR GATE

These gates are purpose-built for confining toddlers but they are an invaluable piece of equipment to have in your home if you own a dog. The gate can be used to confine a puppy or dog to any one room, or to prevent him from going upstairs. It may be necessary to put some wire mesh across the gate when your puppy is quite small, in case he gets his head stuck between the bars. Not only does this frighten the puppy, but it can be difficult to release him.

If your adult dog insists on jumping over the gate when you want him to stay in a particular room, when he has wet feet for example, it is a good idea – especially if it is the doorway between kitchen and lounge – to have a full-height wrought iron gate fitted in place of the door. That way the dog can always see you, but cannot jump out or scratch at the door to have it opened. Be sure that the iron gate does not have patterns within the ironwork that a Beardie could get caught in, and do not leave a collar on your dog in case he should get hooked up on a twirl of the gate pattern.

GARDENS

You must ensure that your garden is a safe place for your Beardie to spend many happy hours in. It will need to be securely fenced with six-feet-high fencing.

Beardies are very agile and can jump quite high when they want to. Be sure that any gates are also high enough and are fitted with substantial Beardie-proof latches.

It is a good idea to have a paved area fenced off in the garden, especially for use in the winter months, so that your Beardie does not come to the back door to be let in wet and covered in mud just before bed-time! Always clear the garden of dog mess, at least once a day, and dispose of it in a suitable manner.

It is not necessary to have a large garden to enable you to keep a dog, provided he has adequate daily exercise. If you have a small garden which has been totally paved, make sure that you have one or two tubs with couch-grass, or similar, growing in them for your Beardie to nibble at when he feels the need. Dogs like to eat grass every now and again to aid their digestive systems and they will often vomit after eating the grass, which is a natural reaction. I have known several dogs who have eaten the fur from their own legs in order to make themselves vomit when there was no grass available.

SWIMMING POOLS

Family pets, as well as children, should not have access to a swimming pool unless supervised. If a dog jumps or falls into a pool which only has a steel ladder for people to climb in and out by, he could eventually die of exhaustion while trying to haul himself out of the steep sides.

A swimming pool with a plastic roll-over cover can be a death-trap to a dog. He does not realise that it is not rigid and may think that he can walk across the cover, which would probably give way under his weight allowing him to sink into the water and become trapped underneath.

3
Caring For Your Puppy

At last, the big day arrives, and it is time to collect your puppy. If possible, take a friend or family member with you to help. Reputable breeders will send you home with a diet sheet, advice on grooming, and some soaked food ready for when you get home. It is an exciting day and you will not remember everything you are told, so make notes, or be sure that the breeder gives you an information sheet that covers most of the things you will need to know about looking after your puppy.

You need to take with you a puppy collar and lead, two towels, kitchen paper, plastic carrier bags, water and a bowl.

TRAVELLING
When I know a puppy will be travelling I do not give him much food, if any, on the day he will be leaving home, depending on the time of day he goes. Hopefully the puppy will not feel travel-sick, and, if you take sensible precautions in the early days, you may be able to avoid travel sickness problems in the future. The puppy should be as far forward in the car as possible, so it is a good idea for him to travel on the lap of the front seat passenger. Sit him on a towel in case of 'accidents'. It is advisable to open the windows a little to let in as much fresh air as possible.

On a long journey it will be necessary to stop to give the puppy time to go to the toilet, and have a drink. Try to find a quiet country spot for this purpose, as the puppy could be upset by traffic noise and, if he is only eight weeks old, he will not yet have had his vaccinations so must not be exercised on ground where other dogs may have been. Although the puppy will not yet be used to a collar and lead, he should have one on so that he cannot run off when you put him on the ground to spend a penny. If you have an estate car you could, at this point, put the puppy in the back of the car with a bowl containing a little water while you have a short break before continuing the journey. When you set off again, return the puppy to the lap of the front seat passenger.

When a puppy can travel happily in the front on someone's lap he can then be put on the back seat, beside a passenger who can reassure him when necessary. Once accustomed to this position, he can progress to sitting on the back seat by himself, and from there can be moved into the tail-gate section of your estate car or hatchback. The object of the exercise is to progress one stage at a time. This can take from a few weeks to a few months until the dog is travelling well where you want him to be in the car.

Useful tip: Try to arrive home in time to give your puppy several hours to get used to his new surroundings, to have some food, a play and a sleep. This will give him the chance to wake up for the first time in his new home, and find that you are there, before it is time to put him to bed for the first night.

ARRIVING HOME

When you arrive home with your puppy, do try to keep the family excitement toned down. He has not long left his mother and littermates, and the home he has known since birth, and will be feeling bewildered. Now the time has come for him to step out into the big wide world on his own four fluffy paws, and he has much to learn!

Let your puppy into the garden to stretch his legs after the journey and to relieve himself. It is a good idea if he is accompanied by the person who looked after him on the trip home. This should help to reassure the puppy as he explores his new

Your puppy will feel bewildered when he first arrives home.

surroundings. The pup should be encouraged to relieve himself in the area that has been designated as his toilet area.

Give your pup a chance to explore the garden.

Once he has had the opportunity to meet the family, including any other dogs and cats, plus time to play and explore his new home, give him a meal, offer him a drink and let him into the garden once more to go to the toilet. Then take him to a quiet area in the house that has been allocated for him. You will have this area prepared with his bed, bedding, a bowl of water, one or two suitable toys, and some sheets of newspaper spread on the floor in case of a mishap.

When prospective owners come to visit their puppy, prior to him leaving home, I encourage them to leave a blanket with me to put in with the puppies. This will pick up the scent of littermates and familiar surroundings and go to his new home with the puppy. The blanket can be placed in the puppy's bed at his new home and should help him to settle in.

Now leave the puppy to rest. Puppies need a lot of sleep for the first few months, and it is most important that when they have had enough playtime and socialising with the family, they are allowed to retreat to their quarters to rest. Under no circumstances should children be allowed to pester the puppy constantly. If they do, you will end up with a snappy, bad-tempered dog. You have a responsibility to spend time training both children and dog right from the start, so that they know how to behave and respect each other. Never leave young children unattended with the puppy. Accidents can occur and, if you are not there to supervise, you may never know exactly what happened.

THE FIRST NIGHT

The first night that your puppy spends in his new home will usually be the worst. Try to understand his point of view. He is missing the comfort of his mother and littermates. He is in strange surroundings, with people he does not yet know, so it is up to you to make him feel as secure, comfortable and loved as possible.

After giving him supper, let him out last thing to go to the toilet and have a play, then settle him in his bed with the blanket that has the scent of his littermates on it, and give him some toys. You may wish to leave a radio on at low volume, to give him company.

If he cries, let him know that you are around, so that he does not feel he has been left totally alone in the big wide world to fend for himself. It may mean getting up a few times in the night to comfort him, but settle him down again and go back to bed. He will soon learn the routine and, come morning, he will be in the starting blocks, with a look of bright anticipation on his face.

PUPPY FEEDING

The breeder will no doubt give you a diet sheet and some food to take home for, at least, the first few meals. It is best to keep the puppy on the diet that has been recommended, but if you do you wish to change this diet in the future it must be done very gradually. Mix a little of the new food into each meal, increasing the amount over two to three days until the changeover is complete.

To begin with, your eight-week-old puppy will be eating four meals a day at 8am, 12noon, 4pm, and 8pm. At 12 weeks, cut out the 4pm feed, and when he is six months old, cut out the midday feed. If you aim to feed only one meal a day eventually, do so at about one year.

Although you are gradually cutting down on the number of meals you give your puppy as he gets older, you must increase the amount of food given at each meal, as he will be going through a stage of rapid growth at this period. By the time he is 18 months old, he should be eating a normal adult diet.

INOCULATIONS

In the UK, dogs are routinely vaccinated against parvovirus, distemper, canine hepatitis, leptospirosis and para-influenza. Protection against rabies is required in some other countries.

To begin with, your puppy will miss the rivalry of his littermates at mealtimes.

Your vet will advise at what age he would like to start a vaccination programme for your puppy. Most begin at eight weeks old, with a follow-up inoculation at 12 weeks of age. Two weeks after the second injection, your puppy should be fully covered against the above diseases and allowed to go to public places and mix with other dogs, but check with your vet first.

Kennel cough is a highly contagious disease which can be dangerous to the young puppy, and older dogs. If your dog ever needs to go into boarding kennels he will need to be vaccinated against kennel cough.

WORMING

All puppies need to be treated for roundworms. The breeder will have already started a worming programme, and will tell you when the next treatment is due. Your vet will give you advice about this when you take the puppy along for his vaccinations.

HOUSE TRAINING

A good deal of patience and vigilance is needed to house train your puppy. The more time you spend on this training, the sooner you will be rewarded. House training is much easier in the spring and summer months, when a door to the garden can usually be left open for most of the day. Hopefully, your puppy will make his own way outside to go to the toilet if you have not been quick enough to notice that he needed to go out.

Do remember that, as soon as your puppy wakes up, or after he has eaten a meal, he will need to go out immediately. Take him to the area which has been

When your puppy is a little older, take him out on short trips to visit friends – human and canine!

Your puppy must be confined to the garden until he has completed his inoculation course.

designated as the dog toilet-zone and say "hurry up", "be quick", "be busy", or whatever word you want the puppy to associate with going to the toilet. When the desired result is obtained, say your chosen word once or twice more, and praise the puppy. He will soon learn to associate the command that you give and will go to the toilet when asked.

Most puppies are accustomed to using newspaper and you will find that, if a few sheets of paper are placed on the floor in his area (but away from his sleeping quarters, as he will not like to foul near his bed), he will generally oblige. Then praise the puppy, pick up the wet or dirty paper and replace with some fresh sheets. At this point it may be as well to take the puppy outside to the toilet area to help him make the association that perhaps it would be a good idea if he went there next time.

Repeat the newspaper process, moving the paper nearer to the outside door, over a period of days or weeks. Eventually, the puppy will learn to walk past the paper and go outside. For the slow-to-learn puppy, you may find that a commercial liquid puppy-trainer, available from any good pet shop, will help to teach him where to perform by giving off the right scent.

Take care not to abandon the current daily newspaper, or your weekly magazine, on the living-room floor before you have finished reading it, as your puppy may think it has been placed there for his benefit! I have known this to happen on more than one occasion. As the puppy matures,

he will gradually gain more bladder control and will not need to go out to the toilet so often.

EXERCISE

Do not over-exercise a puppy. While his bones are soft and developing, his exercise needs to be built up gradually. Running free in a good-sized, securely-fenced garden, should be all a puppy needs for the first four months of his life. Do not let children tire a puppy out; exercise and play are important, but so is sleep.

Prior to your puppy going out for proper walks, do take him out for socialising trips, to visit family and friends who also have a secure garden, where he can play and explore new surroundings. It is also important to introduce him to traffic noise. "Slow but sure" is the motto – do not expect him to take on board too many new experiences all at once. Do not allow a young puppy to jump into and out of estate cars or hatchbacks – he could seriously damage his joints.

At about five months, you can begin to give him short daily walks on his collar and lead. Bear in mind that once the lead goes on, you determine how much exercise the puppy will have and he has no option but to walk with you, so do not overdo things at this stage. As he grows, you can increase the length of time and distance that you walk.

DOS AND DON'TS

Do not throw sticks for a dog. If the stick should land like a lance, and the dog arrives at great speed to retrieve it, there is the great possibility that the end sticking out of the ground may pierce the roof of his mouth and could cause untold damage.

Do not throw, or give, a fir-cone to a dog, as it can lodge in the throat. As it gets moist, the cone opens out and can get stuck, choking the dog.

Do throw a rubber ring, a good-sized ball, or a ragger for your dog to retrieve if you wish.

Establish a routine, and your puppy will soon settle and become an integral member of the family.

Do not give small bones to your dog. Bones are excellent for a puppy to.teethe on and for helping to keep his teeth clean as an adult, but they must be of the correct type for safety.

Do buy sterilised, smoked or roasted bones from a pet shop. Fresh marrow bones are available from some butchers shops. Feed these raw or cook them at home. Marrow can cause an upset stomach in some dogs, so I generally take this out before giving the bones to the dogs. If a bone begins to break up into small or sharp pieces, take it away from your dog.

Do not give old shoes or slippers to your dog. You cannot expect him to know the difference between your new expensive pair and the old discarded ones. If shoes or slippers get chewed by the dog, it is your fault for not putting them out of harm's way.

Do give rawhide chews if you wish, but only in moderation. Be sure that they are of a reasonable size and that you keep an eye on the dog while he has one.

Do not let your puppy, or dog, chew plastic flower-pots, as a piece of plastic can easily get stuck in his gut, with fatal results. Equally, empty plastic bottles or containers are not suitable toys as, not only do they have the same dangers as plastic flower-pots, but they also wear the dog's teeth down.

Do be sensible about what you allow your Beardie to have for toys. In my experience, many Beardies have a favourite toy which they sometimes keep for years. It seems to disappear if a visiting dog comes to stay and miraculously re-appears when the dog has gone home!

4 The Adult Beardie

There are many types of excellent foods on the market, and, once you find one of the correct protein level which your dog enjoys, and that suits his digestive system, stick to it. Dogs are not like humans – they cannot eat something different every day without it upsetting their stomachs.

The feeding instructions on cans or packets are purely guidelines set by the manufacturers, and not hard and fast rules. As with humans, some dogs gain weight readily, while others need extra rations if they are very active and burn up the calories rapidly, so please feed your dog sensibly. Never lose sight of the fact that Bearded Collies are lean, active dogs. You may be surprised to find, under their woolly exterior, how lightly built they are, possessing neither the cobbyness nor the broader build of the Old English Sheepdog. A healthy Beardie will feel firm and well-muscled to the touch. There should be a good covering of flesh over his whole body, but you should be able to feel his ribs, and he should appear to have a waistline. Do not feed tidbits – it is not necessary to do this in order to make your Beardie like you! Take him for walks, give him companionship and he will love you more than if you feed him treats.

FEEDING TIPS
The following tips may be useful:

- Some dogs eat more slowly than others, so if you own more than one dog, feed them separately.
- Never leave food down for more than, say, 20 minutes at meal times, or you will encourage your Beardie to become a fussy eater.
- Teething can cause a dog to go off his food for a while, because the gums become sore at this time. Once he has cut his new

teeth, his appetite should soon return.

• Many Beardies have sensitive digestive systems. If your dog persistently gets an upset stomach, change his diet to one of a lower protein level and, if necessary, offer him two or three smaller meals each day. If the problem persists, seek veterinary advice.

• If your dog is convalescing after illness, he should be kept on a light diet consisting of boiled white fish or chicken with all the bones removed, and boiled rice or pasta added. His normal diet should be re-introduced gradually.

• Never feed your dog just before, or soon after, exercise as he could get bloat. My dogs always return from exercise at least one hour prior to their main meal of the day.

• Special care should be taken in the summer months to cover food that is being prepared for your dog, to prevent flies laying their eggs in it.

COMPLETE FOODS

This type of food is normally sold by the sack. It comes in expanded biscuit, pellet or flaked form. All the vitamins, minerals and trace elements that your dog requires for a balanced diet are included, so

A healthy Beardie should feel firm and well-muscled.

it is not necessary to add further supplements to his diet.

Complete foods can be fed dry, or soaked in water for about 20–30 minutes before offering it to your dog. Try both ways to see which your dog prefers. It is particularly important that, if fed dry, plenty of fresh drinking water is available for your dog. Any soaked food that is not eaten should be thrown away as, if the food is left about for too long, it can start to ferment and cause problems if the dog eats it at this stage.

Complete foods are now manufactured to suit dogs of all ages and lifestyles – Puppy, Junior, Maintenance, Working Dogs, Low Protein for overweight dogs, gluten-free and prescription diets for dogs with a particular health problem. Obviously, the prescription diets are only available from the vet, and fed under his direction.

CANNED FOODS

Do choose a good-quality brand of canned food, as the contents do vary in quality and cheaper brands very often contain large quantities of jelly and cereal, which may not provide a well-balanced diet for your dog.

Canned meat is normally fed with biscuit mixer, thus providing a very tasty, well-balanced diet. Here again, the necessary vitamins and minerals will have been included by the manufacturers, so you will not need to add anything to this meat and biscuit diet.

VACUUM-PACKED FOODS

Vacuum-packed foods usually contain cooked meat or tripe. Some of these foods are complete and others require a mixer biscuit to be added. The packets do not require refrigerating, but once opened you should treat them as cooked meat.

TRADITIONAL FEEDING

Traditional food for your dog consists of fresh or frozen tripe purchased from a pet food supplier (not to be confused with the bleached tripe sold by butchers) and fresh or frozen meat, plus wholemeal biscuit or a mixer. It is always advisable to cook raw meat before feeding it to your dog.

A traditional diet will require the addition of a good vitamin and mineral supplement, in order to ensure your Beardie is getting a well-balanced diet.

EXERCISE

As a rough guide, an adult Beardie usually requires at least one hour of exercise a day – whatever the weather. Do not forget that your Beardie was originally bred to work, and needs mental stimulation as much as exercise. Give him a combination of free-running and road-walking exercise. The road-walking will not only help to keep him – and you – toned up, but it should keep his nails short and the hair on his feet and between his pads worn down nicely.

Beardies love variety in their walks, so try to go to different places. Do not let every car journey finish with a walk, or you may end up with a really excitable dog, who barks continually while

The Beardie will need at least one hour of exercise a day.

in transit, in anticipation of a wonderful free run at the end of the trip. This habit can be very hard to break, so avoid the pitfalls at the beginning by taking your puppy for drives in the car which do not include a stop for a run.

If you go for a walk on the beach and your Beardie has a swim, or a paddle in the sea, wash him down with fresh water when you get home, as salt water left in his coat not only makes it feel sticky, but will also make the hair brittle. Beware of cliff-top walks if your Beardie is not on a lead, as dogs do not always realise that there is a sheer drop looming over the horizon and may fall over the

edge. It is better to be safe than sorry, so keep him on the lead if you are walking somewhere like this.

Although you may like your Beardie to accompany the family on most of its outings, on a really hot day it would be much kinder to the dog to let him stay at home, and ask a friend to take him for a walk. Never leave your Beardie in the car on a hot day. Even with the windows open a few inches, a stationary car can heat to oven temperatures in a matter of minutes, and it would not take long for your dog to die of heat exhaustion, if not rescued and treated in time.

Try to avoid exercising your Beardie in long grass, or near cornfields in the summer, as the grass seeds or corn ears can be a real hazard if they get into the Beardie's skin, or go down his ear. Always check your dog thoroughly when returning from a walk, especially if you have been near thistles or grass seeds. Brush out any debris and check between toes, in ears, under tail, around the groin and armpits. If he has muddy feet, wash off the mud from around the base of the nails, and between the toes, in plenty of lukewarm water, and then leave him to dry on one or two doggy towels for about 15 minutes. Do not let the mud remain on the dog's feet to dry off because it will take longer to dry, and the mud which remains between the toes and around the base of the nails

could result in sores. The same washing process should be carried out in snowy or icy conditions. Snow can collect in balls on the dog's coat, especially the legs, and needs to be melted off in warm water. The salt, plus its chemical mixture, that is used to grit roads really stings the dog's feet, so they will need to be washed thoroughly after the walk. When returning from a walk, make it your habit to clean up the dog before you put the kettle on!

Always take a few plastic bags in your pocket to clean up after your Beardie, as there is absolutely no excuse for dogs' faeces being left in public places. Be a responsible dog owner and always clean up after your dog. It goes without saying that your dog should never be allowed to worry livestock. If there are animals about, put your dog on a lead.

THE IN-SEASON BITCH

Bitches come into season approximately every six months. The season will usually last for about twenty-one days and, at this time, the bitch will have a discharge. This can be messy, but most bitches keep themselves clean. While in season a bitch will need to be kept away from male dogs, even while being exercised – especially around her 10th-18th day, when she will be at her most interesting to the male dogs. Be sure that she cannot get out of the garden and that no straying males, who may have picked up her scent, can get in. Some bitches may decide to go off by themselves to find a mate, so be sure that she is left alone only in a secure place.

If you do not plan to breed, it may be a good idea to have your bitch spayed, but this operation should not be carried out until she is fully mature, after she has had at least one season, and preferably two. If you do decide to have your bitch spayed, it is very important to have this done at a particular point in her breeding cycle. The timing of this operation should be mid-way between her seasons. So, for example, if she comes into season every six months, count twelve weeks from day one of a season and that will be exactly

Breeding a litter is a big responsibility and should not be undertaken lightly.

mid-way between one season and the next. If you get the timing right, there should be minimal, or no, hormone imbalance, to cause any possible problems to your bitch in the future. Here again, my advice would be for you to consult your vet.

BREEDING

Breeders have a duty to do their very best to produce Beardies that are typical, sound and healthy. This can only be achieved by selective breeding. There is a saying: "Mate the best to the best, and hope for the best!" Breeding is a major project, which should not be entered into lightly. It will be necessary to gather information on stud dogs, brood bitches, pedigrees, the care of a bitch in whelp, whelping, equipment, rearing a litter, selling puppies, advice to new owners and, above all, on being able to take a dog back that you have bred, should the situation arise at any time during its life.

Breeding a litter can be an absolute delight, but it is not always straightforward and there can be many pitfalls with much heartache, so please consider all aspects thoroughly, and be sure you are aware what you are taking on if you do decide to breed from your beloved Beardie.

If you show your Beardie, you will be aware of his quality, because you will regularly receive judges' opinions of your dog. It does not always follow that, because your Beardie is merely a pet, he is not of champion quality, but unless he is shown you cannot assess his quality, and will not be able to evaluate how good a specimen of the breed he is.

I would recommend that you attend one or two breed club events, where several breed championship show judges will no doubt be in attendance. Ask two or three of these people to give you an independent assessment of your Beardie, and explain that you may wish to use the dog for breeding. Then see what the consensus of opinion is. If the experts consider your Beardie good enough to breed from, you should then have him X-rayed for hip dysplasia to be sure that his hip status is satisfactory before going any further.

If you intend to show your Bearded Collie he, or she, should not be neutered. If the operation needs to be carried out for veterinary reasons, the Kennel Club should be informed, and the necessary permission granted for the Beardie to continue to be shown afterwards.

CARE OF THE VETERAN

All through his life, your Beardie has done his very best for you. Now, in his old age, it is your turn to repay him with the best possible care and to ensure that you never neglect him in favour of a younger dog. Older dogs can be hard work to care for as, with age, everything begins to slow down. For some, old age may begin at eight years, while others do not start to slow down noticeably until 11-12 years of age. Many Beardies live to the ripe old age of 16 years, and over.

Your Beardie's sight and hearing may become impaired as he gets older, which will make him less responsive to your commands. He may also have stiffness in his joints, making movement slower, but it is still very important to give him regular exercise and mental stimulation. Although it is nice to let him exercise off the lead, at his own pace, if he is hard of hearing he may keep heading off in the wrong direction! In this case it is advisable to keep him on a lead, but do not overdo things as exercise on a lead is forced work. Short walks once or twice a day may be sufficient for some, while others may still be able to go quite a long way.

Your older dog will also enjoy drives in the car to give him a change of scenery, and to make him feel included and a much-loved member of the family.

Useful tip: Keep a bell on the collar of an aged Beardie who has become hard of hearing – if he cannot find you, you will be able to hear where he is!

Your old faithful needs to be regularly groomed. The skin does tend to become more sensitive with age, so be gentle but

The veteran Beardie deserves special care and consideration.

thorough with the grooming and never be in a hurry, using this time to check for any lumps or sores that may need attention. Cut the toenails, which grow more rapidly on an older dog who cannot take so much exercise, and keep his teeth clean, while checking for any that are rotten, which may need to be removed.

Older dogs seem to be obsessed with food, and meal times become the highlight of their day! Divide the meal in half so that he can be fed twice a day, but do not increase the quantity given. It is very important not to let him get fat. Do not feed tidbits and, if necessary, ask your vet about a low-calorie diet for him.

Keep your Beardie smelling sweet by giving him an occasional bath. Be sure to give him a comfortable, warm bed, and always dry him off thoroughly if he should get wet. An annual check at the vet when he goes for his booster injection is always a good idea.

Have patience and understanding for your old friend who has put his trust in you and served you well – now is the time to give him love and serve him well until the end.

EUTHANASIA

When a dog comes to the end of his life, we all hope that he will pass peacefully away in the night, curled up in his favourite bed. Unfortunately, this does not happen very often and we have to be strong and make the decision to have the dog put to sleep. If you feel that your Beardie has lost quality of life because of an incurable illness, or old age, speak to your vet and put your trust in him. No responsible vet likes to put a dog to sleep unless it is absolutely necessary.

Once the decision has been made, make it as easy as possible by calling the vet to your home, so that the dog can be relaxed in his own surroundings. The final procedure must be carried out with sensitivity, to give the dog a dignified end. Hold and comfort your dog while the final injection is given and he slips peacefully away.

Once the great sadness of losing a 'best friend' eases a little, the memories of many happy times spent together during the dog's life will gradually return, and you can have peace of mind knowing that you did not prolong his suffering at the end.

5 Training Your Beardie

The indoor portable kennel is an invaluable item of equipment. If you start using it as soon as your puppy arrives home, you will find it has many uses which will help with your training programme.

• *To sleep in at night as an aid to your puppy's house training* .
Set up the kennel with the puppy's bedding, his toys, and a bowl of water at one end. It is important that he always has a drink of fresh water available. A special water bowl is available that clips on the wire inside the kennel at a height to suit the puppy. Place a few sheets of newspaper at the other end of the kennel, in case he has a mishap.

Last thing at night, before the family go to bed, put the puppy in the garden to relieve himself, then put him to bed in the kennel. Your puppy will not want to foul near his bed, so he will generally bark to be let out to go to the toilet in the morning. Do not reprimand him if he does relieve himself before you get him into the garden. You will be woken quite early for the first few weeks or months, but he will gradually sleep longer as he gets older, and he will also gain more bladder control. At this point he will no longer need to be confined to the kennel at night. He may well choose to continue to sleep in it but, if he does, do not close the door on him, so that he can come and go as he pleases.

• *To keep the puppy away from temptation during his teething stage.*
When the puppy is teething at about 4-6 months of age, anything that stays still, and is chewable, will be a temptation to him. So when you want to go shopping, or leave him unattended in the house for a short period of time, put him in the kennel with something he can chew on, such as a sterilised marrow-bone.

If your puppy is introduced to the indoor kennel at an early stage, he will learn to regard it as a safe haven.

Useful tip: If your table has wooden legs that the puppy may try to chew, buy some rigid plastic piping of the correct diameter from your builder's merchant, cut into suitable lengths, and drop each table-leg into a section of pipe. The puppy may try to chew the pipe but the table legs should be left intact!

• *To put your Beardie in during his meal times.*
This is especially useful if he is a slow eater, or when there is another dog in the household who bolts his own food so that he can steal the puppy's dinner. Such behaviour could cause annoyance. I always feed my dogs separately.

• *As a drying-off area.*
After washing your Beardie's feet when he has returned from a muddy walk, put him in the kennel for about 15 minutes, on some dog towels, to dry. This saves the bother of rubbing legs dry, and stops too many knots forming in the hair on the legs. Once the dog has dried off a little he can then rejoin the family, without leaving wet footprints all around the house.

• *As a recovery room.*
Your Beardie may need to be confined for medical reasons. If he sustains a muscular injury, or for post-operative care, when he must

not be allowed to jump up on anyone or anything in case his stitches get pulled, the kennel is an ideal place for him to rest in. When he comes out, he can be kept on a lead so that you can give him measured amounts of exercise, until he reaches full recovery.

● *To keep your dog away from visitors.*
If a frail, or aged, friend or relation comes to visit, they may find the Beardie's boisterous welcome somewhat overwhelming. Beardies hate being shut away from where the action is, so set up the kennel where both he and the visitor can see each other, and by confining him, his presence will not be too overpowering.

● *As a sanctuary for an aged dog.*
As the years go by – many Beardies reach the ripe old age of 15 or 16 years – your dog may become incontinent. If he has been used to sleeping beside your bed, he may not take too kindly to being put in the kitchen to sleep. He would probably bark to let you know that he was not happy about the situation and nobody would get any sleep. You could

erect the folding kennel in your bedroom and let the dog sleep there. As there is a plastic tray in the bottom, your carpets would not get soiled and your old, faithful Beardie can sleep happily where he always has.

● *For use when on holiday.*
When staying in a hotel that takes dogs, I take my folding kennel, so that my Beardie can be in the room with me, rather than having to stay outside in the car. The dog can stay safely in the kennel while I go to have supper, and I can relax knowing that he cannot get up to mischief while left unattended. On my return I let him out of the kennel, as long as I am there to supervise him. This arrangement is one that most hotels are in favour of.

● *As a grooming table.*
A thick cover put on top of the wire kennel allows it to double up as an ideal table on which to groom your Beardie. If you put him on it from an early age, he will learn to stay up there happily while you brush and comb him.

● *In the car.*
Many people use a folding kennel,

erected in their car, to transport their Beardie safely. In my experience, a kennel which would fit into a car is not large enough for the uses that I have listed above. Therefore, if you want to have one in the car, you would need to buy another for use in the home.

For home use I would recommend a kennel approximately 45 ins x 27 ins x 30 ins high (110cm x 68cm x 76cm).

LEAD TRAINING

The first few times you attach a nylon lead to the puppy's collar, just let him walk around with the lead trailing. When he treads on it, there will be a slight tug on the collar and, when he walks forward, it will become free. This

When you start lead training, allow your puppy to wander around with the lead trailing.

will get him used to something being attached to his neck, without the restriction of a person holding on to the lead and pulling. Repeat this process a few times, under supervision, when there is nobody else around who may step on the lead inadvertently. You can then begin to hold the lead and, with gentle encouragement, the puppy should learn to accept walking on his lead without fighting it.

CHECK-COLLARS

Check-collars do have their uses for training, but you must learn how to use them correctly. They can make a dog pull against you more if not used in the right manner. Never let a dog run loose wearing a check-collar, as they act like a noose if the dog gets caught up in anything, and he could be seriously hurt, or even hang himself. Excessive use of a check-collar will remove all the hair around a Beardie's neck, so if you really feel it is necessary to use one on your dog, then I suggest you buy a leather one, with large rings at each end. If the rings are small, hair can get wrapped around them, preventing the collar being released, so that it stays tight around the dog's neck.

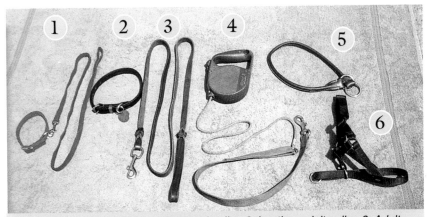

Training equipment: 1. Puppy lead and collar. 2. Leather adult collar. 3. Adult lead. 4. Extending lead. 5. Leather slip collar. 6. Halti.

HALTI™

The Halti is very useful for dogs who are incessant pullers. It looks very much like a horse's head-collar, and has a similar function, allowing you to turn his head towards you when he begins to pull. In this position, he cannot push forward with all of his bodyweight against you.

Once the Halti has been fitted on to the dog correctly, I clip the lead on to the Halti, and also on to the ring of the dog's flat leather collar. This prevents the Halti coming off over the dog's head, should he go into reverse gear. The Halti should be taken off when you let the dog loose for his free-running exercise.

FLEXIBLE LEAD

I have found these extending leads particularly useful for a dog with a pulled muscle, for instance. The dog can be taken out alone to start

The Halti is useful for correcting incessant pullers.

building-up exercise, prior to his being allowed to run free once again. These leads are also invaluable if you have an older dog who is becoming hard of hearing and insists on heading off in the wrong direction when let off his lead!

Care must be taken when your Beardie is on a flexi-lead if you are walking along a pavement. If he is 30 feet ahead of you, he could also go 30 feet sideways and get into the road. If you are using one of these leads, fully extended, when other dogs are running around, the loose dogs do not always see the thin nylon line and can get hurt if they run into it at speed. So, although these leads do have their uses, they must be used sensibly.

BASIC TRAINING

Once your Beardie is old enough, it is a good idea to enrol at a local puppy socialisation class, before progressing to basic obedience. Everything you teach should be well within your puppy's capabilities, so that he can feel proud of his achievements without any strain. Most Beardies do not really enjoy going round and round in a hall doing close heel-work, but I feel it is essential to

The Sit command can be taught by applying pressure to the hindquarters, or by holding a tidbit above the dog's head.

learn how to teach your dog the following basic commands.

"**SIT**": This command is self-explanatory.
"**DOWN**": Means lie flat on the floor or ground. Never give the command "Sit down" as "Sit" and "Down" are two different commands. The dog can only obey one command at a time. In an emergency, "Down" can be a life-saving command if you see an accident about to happen. By being able to get your dog to go down on command, the accident may well be avoided.

"**OFF**": I use the command "Off" when a dog jumps up at me, or puts his front feet up on the kitchen work surfaces or, perhaps, jumps on furniture with wet feet. I do not use the command "Down" in these circumstances, as I do not necessarily want the dog to lie on the floor, but I do want him to put all four feet on the ground! You need to learn the difference between "Sit", "Down", and "Off" in order to teach your Beardie these three totally different commands.

"Down" is one of the most important commands to learn.

"**WAIT**": This asks the dog to stay still until a further command is given. The dog will learn that another command will follow, and that he is going to be asked to do something else.

"Wait" means the dog must stay until the next command is given.

"**STAY**": This tells the dog to "stay there until I come back to you." It is a command that can even be used when you go out shopping leaving the dog at home. Praise the dog when you get back.

"**LEAVE**": This command is a very important one to learn. It could be that another dog is about to bite your dog unless he turns away in time, or your Beardie may be investigating a poisoned, dead

"Stay" means the dog must stay in place until you return.

animal that you do not want him to pick up.

"**COME**": When you call your Reardie, he should learn to return to you wherever you are. When training a puppy, give a reward when he returns to you (dried cat food has an inviting smell and is a convenient reward food). As the dog grows older a pat and verbal reward is sufficient – do not keep feeding tidbits. When your puppy comes to you, make a fuss of him, and then let him go and play again. Put a lead on him for a few minutes now and again, and then let him loose. If you do not do this, you will find that the dog soon learns, especially on a walk, that you only call him when you want to put the lead on to go home. Therefore, when training at home, or out on a walk, it is most important to call the dog to you several times – putting the lead on for a while at times – before letting him loose again, always giving a pat and verbal reward when he returns to you.

If the dog is trained in this way, there should be no problem catching him when the walk ends and you want to head for home.

"**NO**": This is self-explanatory but

Training sessions should always be fun.

try not to use the word too often.

Dogs respect the tone of voice, so lift the voice for praise and deepen it for giving commands.

Dogs do not reason. They will not think "if I sit here she will give me a treat." They must learn, that when they have obeyed, a treat comes!

TRAINING CLASSES

Obedience classes are an excellent socialisation process for your Beardie, but bear in mind that the instructor is there to teach you to train your dog, not to train the dog for you. Endeavour to find a training club that understands the breed (your vet or other dog

Beardievale Village Gossip CD Ex; The Beardie's working ability can be assessed in Working Instinct Tests.

Ch. Deedledee Carefree Rupert: Beardies love competing in Agility.

owners may be able to help), and where the instructor will be sympathetic to the level of training required for you and your dog. Bearded Collies, on the whole, have a gentle nature and do not take kindly to hard handling. Your dog will definitely not concentrate on you, and what you are trying to teach him, in a noisy, hyped-up atmosphere.

Firm, but kind and calm, is the key to training. Always be consistent with the commands you give and be sure that your dog understands what is expected of him. Use the dog's name to gain his attention, and then give the command. Long sentences will only confuse the dog. Do not say "Daisy, come here to me and hurry up. That's a clever girl, come here to me." Do say "Daisy come", and when she does come to you, give gentle praise, such as "Good girl".

WORKING TESTS

In order to preserve the working ability of the Bearded Collie, the breed clubs have devised non-competitive Working Instinct Tests for dogs and owners to work towards. There are four grades of test beginning with basic obedience, progressing through to a higher level, which incorporates tasks that would have been all in a day's work for the original working dog.

The club secretary will be able to give you details of training days which are organised, by the clubs, for owners who would like assistance in training their dogs for the tests. The training days are friendly, informal gatherings which are also very informative. Working Instinct Test Days, where sheep or geese are used to test the Bearded Collie's natural herding and droving abilities, are held once or twice a year by the breed clubs.

AGILITY

The personality of the Bearded Collie makes him the ideal dog for competing in agility. Your dog needs to be trained in basic obedience before embarking on agility and should certainly not be asked to do too much jumping until his bones and muscles are mature at about 18 months to two years of age. It would also be a good idea to have the dog's hips X-rayed for hip dysplasia before starting anything too strenuous.

SHOWING

If you decide to show your Beardie, you will need to find a

training class that specialises in preparing dogs for the show ring. These classes are normally called 'Ringcraft'. Forthcoming shows are advertised in the weekly dog papers which are on sale at large newsagents. Contact the show secretaries for schedules, fill in the entry forms, and return them to the appropriate secretary.

SUMMARY

Even if you do not wish to take part in competitions you can enjoy training your Beardie, just for the fun of it. Several Bearded Collies have achieved great things, both in the show ring as well as in Obedience/Working Trials, which clearly demonstrates the versatility of the breed.

Their boisterous nature means that Beardies take quite a while to train, but, if you put in the time and effort, your reward will be a dog who will be a credit to you, a joy to own, and a pleasure to take anywhere. Untrained, he could become an unruly hooligan through no fault of his own, that you may consider parting company with. Perhaps he would end up being passed from one home to another because of his bad behaviour – who knows how the story would end?

The training of your Beardie is down to you. Learn how to make a good job of it, enjoy it – be sure your dog enjoys it also – and be proud to own an obedient dog.

6 *Grooming*

If you take on a Bearded Collie, you will no doubt have been drawn to the breed by its wonderful 'shaggy dog' appearance, as well as its lovely character. To keep a Bearded Collie well groomed, so that it has a healthy coat and skin, takes time and dedication – but it should be a pleasurable experience for both dog and owner.

EQUIPMENT
You will need to buy the following items:

• A good-quality nylon and bristle brush, preferably made by Mason & Pearson – popular or junior size. These brushes are manufactured for human use and are available in large department stores, or on one or two stalls at dog shows, but are not available in pet shops.

• Hindes Pin Brush No.6063 – these can be obtained at good pet shops or at shows.

• Wooden-handled comb with long, wide-set metal teeth (available as above).

• Small metal comb, with closely-placed teeth. This comb will be useful for combing out the small knots that form between a Beardie's toes (available as above).

• Plastic handled de-matting rake with a double row of metal teeth in a 'V' formation. These rakes are imported from the USA and are excellent for helping to keep your Beardie free of matting. Ask your breeder where to obtain them in the UK.

• Stainless steel forceps – straight, without lock. Used for plucking excess hair out of the ear canals. These can be purchased at dog shows.

Useful tip: Always put steel forceps in a pocket, to warm the metal for a few minutes before use, so that your dog does not get upset by the cold feel of the steel against the sensitive skin on the inside of his ears.

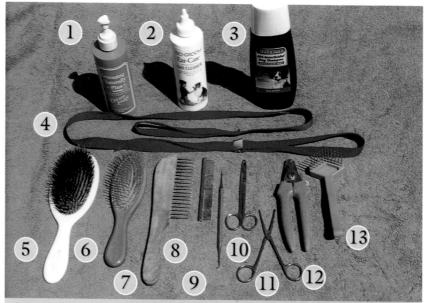

Grooming equipment: 1. Grooming spray. 2. Ear cleaner. 3. Shampoo. 4. Slip lead. 5. Bristle brush. 6. Pin brush. 7. Wooden-handled comb. 8. Metal comb. 9. Tooth descaler. 10. Round-ended scissors. 11. Stainless steel forceps. 12. Nail-clippers. 13. De-matting rake.

• Nail-clippers – Millers Forge 767 stainless steel. These particular nail-clippers looks rather like secateurs that you would use for pruning roses in the garden. I find they give an accurate cut without crushing the nail and enable you to see quite clearly how much nail you are cutting off.
• A good quality anti-static grooming spray which helps the brushes and combs go through the coat more easily and, at the same time, cleans the coat and keeps your Beardie smelling fresh.

• Scissors – a suitable pair of round-ended scissors for keeping your Beardie free of excess hair around his genitals and bottom.
• Tooth descaler – stainless steel, obtainable at shows or some good pet shops.

ROUTINE GROOMING

If your Beardie comes to you for some fuss and attention and you send him away because he is smelly, or if the dog is too dirty to be allowed his usual run of the house, then you are failing to take proper care of him.

It is easy to make a Beardie look reasonably smart by surface brushing with a nylon and bristle brush. However, it is essential not to let the coat become matted, which means that thorough grooming, right down to the skin, is necessary on a regular, weekly basis.

Grooming a coated dog is an art, and hopefully, the breeder will have spent some time showing you how to look after your puppy's coat. If you require more tuition, breed clubs often hold grooming demonstrations and, again, your breeder should be able to advise you about joining a club for this purpose.

If you still find difficulty coping with your Beardie's coat, it is better to admit defeat and find a good canine beautician in your area, who is happy to groom and bath your Beardie on a regular basis – say every seven weeks – to keep him sweet-smelling and in good order.

GROOMING YOUR PUPPY

Train your puppy to be groomed before he really needs grooming,

at eight to nine weeks of age when his coat will be short and easy to take care of. Either groom him on an old sheet or blanket specifically designated for the purpose, on the floor, or put him on a table, or the top of his indoor kennel. Be sure that wherever you choose is nice and firm. Anything that wobbles will make him feel insecure and he will want to jump off.

I always give my puppies a toy, or a chewy treat that they do not normally have, so that when I am grooming them they look forward to the grooming session because of the special treat. This also stops them mouthing at the brush and comb while being groomed – a habit that should never be allowed.

Spray the puppy's coat lightly with the grooming spray and brush him through with the nylon and bristle brush. Comb behind his ears and under his elbows. Brush, then comb gently, under his tail and around the groin area. Trim a small amount of hair away under the tail and around the

Accustom your puppy to being groomed from an early age.

genital area for hygiene reasons. Do not cut this hair too short or close to the skin, as the prickly hair can cause irritation. Check his ears, eyes, and nails and finish with a gentle brush-over with the Hindes pin brush which, although not really required on a puppy coat, does get him used to the feel of the brush for later.

When you have finished grooming your puppy, praise him and put him down on the floor – if groomed on a table – making sure all four feet touch the ground before you let him go, as his co-ordination for jumping and springing does not come for a few weeks yet! Put the special treat away until the next grooming session and go out to play for a while. If you groom your Beardie on a regular basis in this way, he will look forward to the sessions and, as his coat grows during the junior stage, necessitating more work and longer time spent on it, he will be accustomed to the routine.

THE ADULT COAT

Lay the dog flat, on his side if possible, as this makes it easier to groom the undercarriage and legs. Lightly spray with the grooming spray, then slowly work your way

Grooming is easier if your dog lies flat on the grooming table.

through the coat with the nylon and bristle brush, one layer at a time, from one end of the dog to the other. Use more spray as required.

Useful tip: Dogs do not like their coats being brushed against the lie of the hair – especially on the legs, so try to flip the hair up and then groom in the direction the hair lays. On the legs, for example, work from the toes to the elbow, but brushing and combing the coat towards the toes.

As each layer is completed, comb through with either the wooden

The de-matting rake is used to tease out tangles.

handled comb or the 'V' shaped rake to ensure that there are no matts in the coat. Gently tease out any matts by holding the matt between the thumb and first finger of one hand, while combing out the matt with the other. Never pull against the dog's skin – only use pressure against the finger and thumb holding the matt. Turn the dog over and repeat the process.

Special attention must be paid to undercarriage, groin area, elbows, armpits, hocks, legs, feet, face and behind the ears. Trim hair lightly under the tail and around genital areas for hygiene reasons. Finish off with a nice brush through with the pin brush. Let your Beardie stand up and have a nice 'head to tail' shake and he can go off to play.

EARS

Check ears and pluck out excess hair with the forceps. Pull out a few hairs at a time, with short sharp tugs and get as near to the roots of the hairs as possible, but do not, under any circumstances, poke the forceps down the ear canal. Clean out any wax deposits from the crevices of the ears with cotton wool and a good quality ear cleaner from the vet or pet shop.

Should your Beardie have an ear infection, or mites in his ears, he will need ear drops to soften and lift wax deposits or infection,

Use an ear-cleaner for wax deposits.

which will then float up the ear canal. Clean out the ears before putting the next drops in, or you will only push the infected debris down again, making it almost impossible to deal with the problem. Repeat the process until the infection clears up totally. Ear infections can be serious and life-threatening – do not hesitate to consult your vet if you are in any doubt.

EYES

If any redness or excess discharge is evident, consult your vet. Always clean the 'sleepy dust' out of the corners of your dog's eyes – this is best done with cotton wool, dampened with water that has been boiled and cooled to blood temperature.

Use moist cotton wool to clean the eyes.

These days many Beardies have a heavier coat than their ancestors. Should your Beardie have a heavy head coat, do not expect him to walk around unable to see the light of day! If he is a pet, trim it to a spikey fringe, or if he is to be shown, fix the hair back out of his eyes with an elastic band until he goes into the ring.

NAILS

Check toenails regularly, not forgetting the dew-claws if they have been left on. Dew-claws are the remains of a fifth toe, positioned on the inside of the front paws, and slightly higher than the other four toes. Because they are higher and not subjected to wear from friction, it is essential they are clipped as short as possible so they do not grow inward and penetrate the dog's skin, or the soft pad behind them.

Remove only the tips of the nails, so as not to cut the quick – which would not only cause pain and bleeding, but persuade the dog not to let you inspect his feet in the future! Always check between the toes and pads for knots, dirt or

Remove the tips of the nails using nail-clippers.

other matter which may have accumulated and be causing discomfort. If your Beardie does develop a nail-bed infection seek advice from your vet.

TEETH

It is most important to keep your dog's teeth clean and in good condition. A correct diet, the right kind of bones to chew, and teeth-cleaning toys to play with, should normally keep teeth clean. But check the teeth on a regular basis for tartar or sore gums.

Excess tartar should be removed with a tooth descaler.

Clean off excess tartar with a tooth descaler, but care must be taken not to jab the dog in the gums. Lay the dog flat on its side, lift the lip to expose the gums and use the descaler, working away from the gums towards the edge of the teeth. If the dog has any rotten teeth or sores on the gums, he will need veterinary treatment. While checking the teeth, make sure that no food has collected in the hair around the mouth, and comb out if necessary.

BATHING

It is not possible to say how often a Bearded Collie should be bathed. Bathing not only helps to keep the coat and skin clean and healthy, but it also helps to make your pet a pleasure to live with. The coat should be thoroughly groomed before the bath to

Apply the shampoo with a sponge.

remove any matting and debris. Never groom knots out of your Bearded Collie when he is wet – it is too painful for the dog, as the knots get tighter in water, and are then very difficult to get out. Hair is more elastic when wet so it is more likely to break.

There are some excellent canine shampoos on the market. Choose one to suit your circumstances – either a conditioning shampoo, special treatment, or insecticidal shampoo. Do not ignore the signs if your Beardie is scratching a lot. Put him in the bath promptly and, if you suspect a flea problem, be sure the label on the shampoo says "kills fleas" and not "controls fleas". The latter may only make the fleas drowsy for half an hour or so, and your efforts would be wasted! Bathing and drying a Beardie correctly is hard work, so be sure that you have the right shampoo for the purpose before

you start and, if your efforts do not stop the dog scratching, it may be best to consult your vet, as a stronger, prescription shampoo may be required.

Check list of items required when bathing the dog:
- Rubber safety mat.
- Plastic jug.
- Sponge.
- Shampoo/conditioner.
- Nylon slip lead.
- Shower-head spray.
- Dog towels or absorbent cloths.
- Plastic apron.

Place the rubber mat in the base of the bath, mix some shampoo with warm water in the jug, place dog towels on the floor for when the dog jumps out after his bath, and put on your apron. Put the nylon slip lead (nylon will not be spoiled by getting wet) on the dog and lead him to the bath. Lift him in gently and, if he will not stand quietly on his own, get someone to hold the lead.

Holding the shower-head spray in your hand, dampen the coat with warm water, but do not get the dog's head wet at this stage.

Rinse the coat thoroughly.

Wipe off excess moisture.

As you dry the coat, brush it through with a bristle brush.

Apply shampoo to the dog's coat with the sponge. Give him a quick rinse then wet and shampoo the head, taking great care not to get shampoo into his eyes.

When rinsing, keep water out of the ears by placing your thumb over the ear opening and the hand over the eyes to prevent soap from getting into them. Be careful not to get water into the dog's nostrils – push his nose gently downwards while rinsing the muzzle. The final rinse must be very thorough in order to get all the soap out of the dog's coat. Remove excess water by gently squeezing the hair on the legs, tail, ears and all parts of the dog's body.

Useful tip: If the dog begins to shake water off himself, place your hand firmly on his head and he will usually stop the "head to tail shake"

If you have bought absorbent cloths for drying, these may be used while the dog is still in the bath. Rub the dog with the cloths, then wring out and re-use like a chamois leather. When the dog feels reasonably towel-dried, invite him to jump out of the bath on to the dog towels, let him have a shake and take him to where he will be dried more thoroughly.

DRYING
Never leave a dog to dry out naturally, unless it is a hot day. Allow enough time to ensure that your dog does not go to bed with more than just damp feet. If you are using a hair-dryer, set on warm and direct the air to one area of the dog's coat at a time. Brush in quick, even strokes with either the nylon and bristle, or pin-brush. Brush the hair upwards, and then downwards, and work on each area until the dog is dry all over.

The finished result.

Health Care

On the whole, the Bearded Collie is a healthy breed, and your dog should live to a reasonable age, with few visits to the vet other than for routine booster inoculations. However, it is important to have a basic knowledge of some of the problems that might be encountered, so that you can spot signs of trouble at an early stage.

TEMPERATURE

If ever you are concerned about your Beardie's health, it is very useful to be able to take his temperature. To do this, stoop down, put one knee under the dog's stomach so that he cannot sit (unless he is lying down), lift the tail, gently insert the thermometer into the dog's rectum, and hold it there for approximately one minute.

A dog's normal temperature is 101.5 degrees Fahenreheit. If it varies too much either side of this temperature, it is advisable to take the dog to the vet immediately. The temperature of a bitch who is about to have puppies drops to 98 degrees F – this is normal. Be sure that the thermometer you use is a stubby-ended traditional type, or a digital thermometer.

GIVING MEDICATION

TABLETS

Tablets are best disguised in a piece of butter, cheese or meat. Sit the dog in front of you and feed it a piece of the chosen food without a tablet in it. For an extra-suspicious Beardie repeat the process! When he is confident that he is only getting tasty treats, put the tablet in the next piece of food. It should be swallowed with no problems if you follow this routine.

When you need to give half a tablet, break it across the middle, damp a finger with water and rub the sharp corner of the tablet with your damp finger. This will round off the sharp edge and reduce the risk of the dog's throat being scratched as he swallows the tablet.

LIQUID MEDICATION

This is best administered with a syringe (minus needle) or dropper. Lift the dog's head up, gently pull a small flap of flesh away from the teeth at one side of the jaw. Quickly slide the syringe into this cheek pocket and empty the medicine. Keeping the dog's head up and his mouth shut, rub the throat gently until he swallows and the medicine goes down. If you open the dog's mouth and squirt the medicine on to his tongue or into the back of his throat, he will just close his throat and spit it back at you!

INOCULATIONS

After your puppy has completed his initial vaccination programme, he will need a booster inoculation every year for the rest of his life. This is also a good opportunity for the vet to give your dog a general check-up.

A-Z OF COMMON AILMENTS

ANAL GLANDS

These are small glands positioned on either side of the anus on the outside surface of the rectum. When these glands require emptying, they fill with a fluid which has a strong, foul-smelling odour. The glands when full often cause the dog irritation and he may nibble at the area or drag his bottom along the ground. Serious damage can occur if an unskilled person attempts to empty the glands, so check the area for odour, swelling or an abscess and, should there be a problem, contact your vet.

BLOAT/TORSION

This occurs when excess gas causes the stomach to swell and the intestine to twist, cutting off both entrance and exit to the stomach, which continues to enlarge. This is a very painful, and life-

affected area with cotton wool and keep in place with Micropore tape. This is an adhesive tape, available at chemist shops, which sticks to itself, but not to hair or skin. Do not wind the tape too tightly around the dog's paw or you may interfere with his circulation. Put a small, strong, plastic bag over the dog's paw and hold this in place with more tape around the top.

Exercise the dog on grass, and on return from the walk, remove bag and padding from the paw to let air to the wound. If the dog prevents the wound from healing by constantly licking it, you may need to obtain an Elizabethan collar from the vet. Remember that a dog cannot eat or drink while wearing one of these collars, so it will need to be removed at intervals when you can keep an eye on him. Seek veterinary advice for severe cuts and badly-torn claws, or if a wound will not heal.

threatening, condition and the dog should be seen by a vet within 30 minutes of the onset of symptoms to give him any chance of survival.

Thankfully, Beardies are not prone to bloat, but to avoid the condition occurring, do not feed your dog less than half-an-hour before, or after, exercise

CUT PADS/TORN CLAWS

Superficial cuts should be bathed three times a day in a saline solution – at a ratio of one level teaspoon of salt to one pint of cooled, boiled water. To enable the dog to be exercised while the wound is healing, pack the

CYSTITIS

Cystitis is caused by inflammation of the bladder resulting from infection. Symptoms are frequent passing of urine and discomfort or straining when doing so. There may be spots of blood present in the urine. Cystitis and vaginitis (inflammation of the vagina)

occur quite frequently in young Beardies. Your vet will need to see the Beardie. Take a small sample of her urine along with you.

Treatment with a course of antibiotics generally clears the problem up promptly.

Useful tip: To collect a urine sample from a Bitch, put her on a lead, wait until she starts to urinate, and slide a flat dish under her from the rear.

Collecting a urine sample from a young dog who still squats would be as above, but slide the flat dish in from the side. To collect a urine sample from an adult male dog follow the example above, but collect the sample in a jug.

DIARRHOEA

If your Beardie has diarrhoea it may indicate nothing more than the result of an error of diet, or a chill. However, it is very important not to feed the dog anything for 24 hours, in which time the stomach will empty and settle down. During this period make sure that plenty of fresh drinking water is available. For the next few days, feed boiled chicken or fish with rice or pasta. Gradually introduce a normal diet

when you feel happy that the problem is resolved. Should the diarrhoea persist, in conjunction with vomiting, or blood, consult your vet without delay.

HEATSTROKE

Never leave your Beardie in the car on a warm day, even if it is overcast and the windows are all open a few inches. The inside of a car can heat to oven temperature within minutes. The body temperature of your dog will soar, and he could suffer heatstroke, which is potentially fatal.

If heatstroke is suspected (the dog will be vomiting, have severe diarrhoea and be in a state of collapse), it is imperative to reduce his body temperature immediately. Either submerge him up to the neck in a bath of cool water, or a river, or hose him down until his temperature is lower. If the dog is in a state of collapse, go to a vet immediately.

HIP DYSPLASIA

Hip dysplasia is a term relating to varying degrees of malformation of the ball and socket joints forming the hips. The condition is found in several breeds, and some are more badly affected than others. On the whole, it is not a

Sallen Rhum at Runival and Quinbury Snowdrifer at Runival CD Ex, a registered search and rescue dog, pictured in the Cairngorms.

major problem with Bearded Collies and careful breeding should ensure that it stays that way. Mild cases may not display any obvious signs of a hip problem, but in severe cases it can show in a puppy as young as five to six months. The puppy may have trouble getting to his feet from a sitting position, and could have difficulty walking.

The condition can only be diagnosed by X-ray and, should you contemplate breeding from your Beardie, your dog must be X-rayed for hip dysplasia to ascertain his hip status. There are different schemes for hip scoring,

depending on where you live. In the UK, the lower the score the less degree of hip dysplasia present. The minimum score, for each hip is 0 and the maximum 53, which gives a total range of 0-106.

KENNEL COUGH

As the name suggests, this highly contagious virus can be common in places where many dogs are housed together, and is transmitted in air-borne particles or by dogs sniffing noses. The first symptom to note is the dog clearing his throat, which many owners mistake for the dog having something stuck in the throat, or by coughing when he is excited, or after exercise.

If you suspect kennel cough, isolate the dog immediately, and consult your vet. If you take the dog to see the vet, do not go into the waiting room but, when it is your turn, go directly into the consulting room, without giving your dog the chance to sniff other dogs on the way in. Antibiotics may be prescribed to prevent secondary chest infection. It is important to keep the dog warm and quiet until symptoms subside. Your Beardie should be vaccinated against kennel cough before staying at a boarding kennel.

PARASITES – INTERNAL

There are two types of worm more commonly found in dogs – roundworm and tapeworm. In other countries, including some areas of the USA, dogs also need treatment for heartworm.

Roundworms: These are primarily a parasite of young puppies, who become infected while still in the womb. It is most important that puppies are wormed from approximately two and a half weeks of age, with a suitable preparation obtained from a vet. They should be wormed again at five weeks, at eight weeks, and 12 weeks Adult dogs should be regularly wormed every three or six months, as natural re-infection will occur.

Tapeworm: As the name suggests, this is a flat ribbon-like worm which consists of a sucking head, (which attaches to the dog's gut), and body segments forming a ribbon, which can grow to several feet in length. As the segments break off they pass out with the dog's faeces and can be seen as rice-like grains around the dog's rectum.

The flea is one of the intermediate hosts of the tapeworm, so if your Beardie has had fleas, it is wise to worm him for tapeworm as a precaution. Tell your vet if you suspect tapeworm and he can supply a worming preparation. You should have an accurate note of your dog's weight to work out the correct dose.

PARASITES – EXTERNAL

External parasites in a shaggy-coated breed can be a real problem. If your Beardie is scratching, give him a thorough examination to establish the cause and take action.

If you cannot find an obvious cause for the dog's continual scratching, take him to the vet. Should the vet prescribe an anti-inflammatory injection, or tablets, to reduce severe irritation, bear in mind that this only masks the problem, and does not cure it.

Fleas: These are small, reddish-brown insects, whose bites cause tremendous irritation to a dog. They can move at great speed through the dog's coat and are often difficult to see. A tell-tale sign that your dog has fleas is the presence of clusters of what appear to be black sand-like grains on the skin which dissolve when placed on a wet, white tissue, leaving a reddish-brown stain. These are flea excreta.

Should your dog have quite a few fleas in his coat, I would give him an insecticidal bath. Spray the dog's bedding and any areas in the house where the dog goes with a good-quality flea spray designed for the purpose, following the manufacturer's instructions. A few days later spray the dog with a good-quality spray from the vet (Do not give the dog an insecticidal bath and insecticidal spray on the same day, but initially a bath may be more effective),

which should stop any fleas from re-infesting the dog for several weeks. Make sure to use one spray for the house and a different type for the dog. Severe infestations can cause anaemia and eczema.

Lice: A louse is another biting insect, but is generally easier to eradicate as, unlike the flea, it cannot jump and is slow-moving. Lice are small with a beige-brown body. They generally gather on a dog's ears and around his neck. The eggs are laid on the dog's hair – combing with a flea comb can help lift the eggs off the hair, which is possible with a puppy while the coat is still short, but in a full-coated Beardie this is impossible.

When giving the dog a suitable insecticidal bath, make sure that you lift off any scabs that have formed. Do this while the dog is in the bath and the scabs have softened. These scabs act as umbrellas to the lice and they can hide underneath them out of reach of the shampoo, so this is a very important point! Repeat the process weekly until the problem is resolved. The house and the dog's bedding should be sprayed at the same time.

Ticks: Ticks are normally more prevalent in sheep and deer country. They are blood-sucking insects which attach themselves to the dog's skin with a biting head. Before they begin to feed they look like a dark brown or black flat-bodied money-spider crawling around, but once their body has engorged with blood they look like a greyish-purple baked bean – and are about the same size! Many people mistake them for a wart to begin with.

There is a knack to successfully removing a tick, without leaving its biting head still buried in the dog's skin, which could result in an abscess forming. The best way to kill and remove a tick is to soak some cotton wool with flea spray and apply liberally to the tick, which should then die and fall off. You may need to make one or two applications of the spray. Take care when removing a tick from around the dog's eyes.

Ticks will eventually fall off the host of their own accord once they are full-up with blood. However, it is not a good idea to wait for this to happen. If the tick does not fall off, hold it as near as possible to its biting head and give a quick *twist* and *pull* action, this should release the tick's biting head, and the whole thing should come free in one piece.

Harvest Mites: As the name suggests, these mites are around in the summer months. They look like minute grains of orange sand and gather in clusters, mainly between the dog's toes and on his eyebrows. Your dog should be washed in an appropriate shampoo, taking care not to get any chemicals in his eyes.

PROSTATE GLAND

When the problem of inflammation of the prostate gland does arise, it is generally in dogs over five years old. The signs to look for are:

- Blood dripping from penis.
- Motions which appear flattened and ribbon-like, due to passing near the inflamed prostate gland when the dog defecates.
- Inability to pass urine.

The retention of urine is life-threatening, and veterinary help should be sought immediately. In the first instance, your vet may try treating the problem with female hormones, which generally reduces the inflammation of the gland, but if the problem recurs, the only permanent solution is castration.

With good care, your Beardie should live to a good age, and suffer few health problems.

PYOMETRA

Pyometra is a condition whereby the bitch's uterus fills with pus. With an open pyometra you will see, and smell, a thick copious brown/cream putrid discharge from the bitch's vagina. The bitch will also have a high temperature and increased thirst.

A closed pyometra differs from above, in that the pus is trapped within the uterus and escapes by seeping through the walls of the uterus and into the bloodstream. By the time you discover that anything is amiss, you have a very sick bitch on your hands. Here again tell-tale symptoms would be increased thirst and a high temperature. Both types of pyometra are life-threatening and require immediate veterinary attention.

STINGS

Discourage your dog from snapping at bees and wasps, but if he does get stung, try to find the sting and pull it out with tweezers. Contact your vet immediately if the dog gets stung in the mouth, and it begins to swell.